Pennies to Dollars
❦ The Story of Maggie Lena Walker ❧

Maggie Lena Walker

Pennies to Dollars

The Story of
❧ Maggie Lena Walker ❧

by

Muriel Miller Branch
and Dorothy Marie Rice

Linnet Books
1997

This thoroughly revised and rewritten edition of *Miss Maggie: A Biography of Maggie Lena Walker* by Muriel Branch and Dorothy Marie Rice (Richmond, Va.: Marlborough House Publishing Co., 1984) is first published 1997 as a Linnet Book, an imprint of The Shoe String Press, Inc., North Haven, Connecticut 06473.

Library of Congress Cataloging-in-Publication Data

Branch, Muriel Miller.
Pennies to dollars: the story of Maggie Lena Walker /
by Muriel Miller Branch and Dorothy Marie Rice.
p.   cm.
Includes index.
Summary: The story of the woman whose life of hard work, perseverance, and resourcefulness enabled her to found the first African-American owned bank in this country.
ISBN 0-208-02453-0 (lib. bdg.: alk. paper).
ISBN 0-208-02455-7 (pbk.: alk. paper).
1. Walker, Maggie Lena, 1867–1934—Juvenile literature.
2. Afro-American women—Virginia—Richmond—Biography—Juvenile literature.   3. Afro-Americans—Virginia—Richmond—Biography—Juvenile literature.   4. Bankers—Virginia—Richmond—Biography—Juvenile literature.   5. Richmond (Va.)—Biography—Juvenile literature.   [1. Walker, Maggie Lena, 1867–1934.   2. Afro-Americans.   3. Bankers.   4. Women—Biography.]   I. Rice, Dorothy Marie, 1948–
II. Title.
F234.R53B73   1997
332.1'2'092—dc21
[B]
97-20280
CIP
AC

The paper in this publication meets the minimum requirements of American National Standard for Information Sciences—Permanence of Paper for Printed Library Materials, ANSI Z39.48—1984.

Printed in the United States of America

To all the strong, courageous black women
who have inspired and nurtured our creativity,
especially our mothers, Missouri and Lucille,
and our aunts, Lillie and Clara.
To Uncle Coolidge, who showed us
that it is okay to laugh and enjoy life;
and to our husbands, Willis and Michael,
for their patience and encouragement.

Contents

Acknowledgments

We are grateful for all persons who have preserved the history of Maggie Lena Mitchell Walker: her grandchildren Maggie Laura, Mamie Evelyn, Armstead, and Elizabeth; The Maggie Walker Historical Foundation; Celia Suggs and other National Park Service personnel who made available to us Mrs. Walker's speeches, oral histories, diaries, photographs, and other archival materials. We also thank Mrs. Dorothy Turner, former Secretary of St. Luke, for her contributions to the first edition of this book. We thank the staffs at the Library of Virginia, the Consolidated Bank and Trust Company, and the Virginia Historical Society. Finally, we appreciate the research done by the late Dr. Gertrude Marlow of Howard University.

All photographs in this book are used courtesy of the National Park Service, Maggie L. Walker National Historic Site.

Authors' Note

The terms "Negro," "colored," "Afro-American," "person of color," and "black" are used in this book to describe African Americans, because they are some of the words that people used during Maggie Lena Walker's life.

Maggie Walker's own words, from her diaries and speeches, are given in italics.

❧ 1 ❧

Humble Beginnings

Ivory magnolia petals and orange honey-suckle blossoms infused the air with their delicate perfumes. Daisies and blue cornflowers swayed in the occasional breeze of the summer day. Cardinals flashed their red wings; robins chirped, and whippoorwills sang on branches. It was July 15, 1867, and Elizabeth Draper, ex-slave, had just given birth to her firstborn: a daughter.

Elizabeth had been freed before the Civil War by the Van Lew family and she had chosen to remain as a house servant on their estate in Richmond, Virginia. As Quakers, the Van Lews did not believe in slavery. They believed that slavery should be abolished. It was a matter of religion and conscience for them.

While in the service of the Van Lews, Elizabeth conceived her daughter Maggie Dalena, who would later be called Maggie Lena, with a white man, Eccles Cuthbert. Cuthbert was an Irish-born newspaperman and a correspondent for the *New York Herald*. Their biracial union was an affront to conventional values of whites, who feared the "amalgamation" of the races. And yet such unions were fairly common in the postwar South. Although he remained in Richmond until 1890, Eccles did not marry Elizabeth. Marriage between Negroes and whites would be illegal in Virginia until 1967.

The midwife wiped sweat from the new mother's brow. She handed her the tiny infant. As the baby suckled from her mother's dark brown breast, Elizabeth Draper looked upon the girl child in her arms, and contemplated the topsy-turvy world into which her baby had been born. As she nursed her daughter and cradled her to sleep, there was one thing of which Elizabeth Draper was most certain: This child would never be a slave.

There is an old wives' tale that says you can see greatness in an infant's eyes. When she looked into the unfocused eyes of her tiny daughter, Elizabeth just knew this child would accomplish great things, this child who would arise from the ashes of a war-torn city. . . .

❧ 2 ❧

War-torn City

Richmond, Virginia, was once a thriving queen of the South, where cotton was king and tobacco was a prince. Its industrial, commercial, and slave markets bustled with high energy. The forging of iron and the selling of human flesh had existed side by side in Richmond. Slavery had driven the engines of the city's success.

Like so many cities and towns in the South in 1867, Richmond was still smoldering from four years of war. It had once been the proud Confederate capital, but now there were only the ruins of a burned city. Although the fires on the battlefields had been extinguished, fires of another kind were still burning in the spirit of the people: former slaves; Confederate families; and Northern abolitionists. All were full of the hope that comes with victory, or the dread that comes with defeat.

Women's petticoats and skirts swept the dirt roads. People scurried on foot; horses clip-clopped; wagons pitched and rolled on cobblestone streets. The air was full of odors and sounds from open sewage, animals roaming, fruit and vegetables fermenting in the humidity; the musk of too many people compressed in a choking city—restless, often homeless people seeking familiar faces.

For the time being, the whole social order had been turned upside-down like a turtle on its shell. After having fought for a cause, and lost, the former Confederate nation was angry and hostile toward their former slaves and the victorious Union government under Abraham Lincoln. On April 15, 1865, just two days after the surrender of Confederate General Robert E. Lee at Appomattox, President Lincoln was assassinated. The Negroes had lost their "Great Emancipator" who had freed them from slavery, but his murder grieved both sides. According to General George E. Pickett, who had led the near-suicidal "Pickett's Charge" against the Northern army at Gettysburg, "The South has lost her best friend and protector in this her direst hour of need."

Southerners had hoped that President Lincoln would have been conciliatory toward them. They did not feel that his successor, President Andrew Johnson, would be able to keep the Northern radicals in check. These radicals were the Republican party members who wanted to make sure the Southern slaves were given all their rights immediately, rather than gradually. The South had been based on an agrarian culture that depended on slave labor. Most of these slaves were illiterate, and had never learned to govern themselves. Many Southerners felt the whole region would be in chaos if ex-slaves had the same rights as the whites.

After a series of political setbacks brought on by the radical Republican party, the ex-Confederate leaders, businessmen, and soldiers were pardoned by President Johnson. It wasn't long after the war that they had recaptured their former prominence. The Southern turtle was being transformed into a fast-moving hare.

Meanwhile, Richmond was writhing in the pains of its rebirth after the war. It was a city occupied by the enemy: Union soldiers. It was now governed as Military District Number One. This temporary arrangement did not work out well, because the white citizens were angry that they had lost their rights, and were not allowed to control their own lives without the approval of the new military government. Anyone who had fought against the Union was not allowed to hold office or to vote. That applied to the majority of white men.

Worse still for these defeated people, the former slaves were now being protected, and given rights that had previously been for whites only. Unfortunately, the former slaves were often mistreated by the white Union officers whose duty was to defend them. There was scattered violence. Freedom had come, but it was a bittersweet victory. Where would the people go? What would they do? The promise of freedom was grander than the daily realities of survival. The "forty acres and a mule" ex-slaves had been told they could have did not materialize either. The freedmen would have to eke out a living and manage their own lives. Could they make it on their own?

Fortunately, the Freedman's Bureau had been set up in 1866, to help feed, protect, and educate the former slaves. Schools were established to teach the illiterate how to read and write. Often parents and children sat side by side,

Elizabeth Draper Mitchell, Maggie's mother, had been a slave. Her hard work and determination to see her children educated had a lasting effect on Maggie.

William Mitchell was Maggie's stepfather. His untimely death would make a great impact on the nine-year-old girl.

learning in the same classroom. The Freedman's Bureau chief in Virginia was the former general O. O. Howard. He would later help establish Howard University, the great African-American university in Washington, D.C.

In 1867, the General Assembly of Virginia had legalized marriages between blacks. Before the war, there had been no legal sanctions, so men and women lived together if they were allowed, usually with their master's consent. All such marriages that had taken place during slavery were now legal and the children born in those marriages were declared legitimate.

And so ten months after Maggie Lena's birth, on May 27, 1868, Elizabeth Draper did marry. She married William Mitchell, a mulatto butler in the Van Lew house. According to Maggie's later diary, *"he was the lightest skinned colored man she could find"* so that people would think he was Maggie's real father. And for the first nine years of her life, he was. Her natural father would reappear in Maggie's life in 1883, around the time of her graduation from Normal School.

❧ 3 ❧

Seeds of Self-help

Elizabeth and William Mitchell moved their family to a two-story clapboard house located in an alley off College Street, near the Medical College of Virginia. It was a far cry from the Van Lew estate on Church Hill, high above the James River. But it was a beginning. William Mitchell held a job as headwaiter at the St. Charles, the most prominent hotel in Richmond at the time. It was located on Main Street, four blocks from his home, and only a block from the Virginia state capitol. Mitchell was fortunate, because after the war, many Negro men were still roaming the city in search of jobs. For them, freedom was becoming a wilted dream. Without food, money, jobs, or family assistance, they had become a public nuisance.

In 1866, the Vagrancy Laws had been passed to discourage homeless Negro men and women

(Top) Maggie's girlhood home was in an alley off College Street in Richmond. It was a far cry from her birthplace, the Van Lew mansion (bottom) which lapsed into decay after the Civil War.

from entering or remaining in the city. These laws, like so many passed in the postwar South to control the movements of the Negro population, were indiscriminately used by whites. In many respects the Vagrancy Laws reinstituted slavery, by restricting the movement of freed men.

Yet, many continued to roam. Some became sick, or starved, and died without even the dignity of a decent burial. Dead bodies cast along the roadsides became a familiar, yet ugly sight. But in the midst of this human tragedy, flickered rays of hope. The African-American mutual benefit societies, which had been illegal before the war, stepped in to assist their brethren. The Daughters of St. Luke was one such organization.

By a stroke of divine coincidence, Maggie Lena was born the same year that an ex-slave, Mary Prout, gave birth to an idea. Determined to comfort people in sickness and to give their deaths some dignity, Prout organized the first Home for Colored Aged Men and Women. A devout and active member of the Bethel African Methodist Church in Baltimore, Maryland, she convinced them to organize the Home there.

These seeds of self-help that Mary Prout had planted germinated and grew into the larger or-

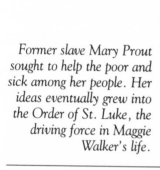

Former slave Mary Prout sought to help the poor and sick among her people. Her ideas eventually grew into the Order of St. Luke, the driving force in Maggie Walker's life.

ganization, the Daughters of St. Luke. It was named for the Apostle Luke in the Bible, a physician who ministered to the sick. In the beginning, only women were allowed to join this secret society, but later men were admitted. As the Order grew and changed, so did its name. It finally became known as the Independent Order of St. Luke. It was to become the driving force in Maggie Lena's life.

❧ 4 ❧

Tragedy and Hard Work

Like so many former slaves, Elizabeth Draper Mitchell used her talents and skills to become self-employed. She became a washerwoman. She rose at dawn. She had to ready the wood stove for the family's breakfast and also begin the tedious task of ironing the clothes that she had washed the day before. Starting the stove was not as simple as turning a knob. It required collecting kindling and firewood and stoking the charcoal to keep the fire hot. This work had to be done in the humid heat of summer as well as the damp, cold winter. Her work was not easy. Her son Johnnie had been born in 1870. In addition to her housekeeping chores and laundry work, she now had two children to care for.

Meanwhile, William Mitchell got ready each day to begin his daily trek to the St. Charles Hotel. When he arrived, he put on his jacket, carefully fastened his buttons, and viewed himself in the mirror. Confident that he had passed his personal inspection, he began his duties. As headwaiter, he was responsible for supervising the other waiters and making sure that the guests were served promptly and satisfactorily.

Then one evening in February 1876, William Mitchell did not return home as usual. Maggie noticed her mother impatiently pacing the floor. She saw the worried look etched on her mother's face. By the next morning, Elizabeth's worry had been replaced by a fear so great Maggie could feel it. Together they scoured the streets frantically, asking neighbors if they had seen William Mitchell or knew of his whereabouts. No one had seen him. Rumors flew like feathers in a henhouse.

Finally, five days after the disappearance and the frantic search had begun, William Mitchell's body was pulled from the James River. When the coroner specified suicide by drowning, his wife refused to believe it. Elizabeth thought that her husband had been murdered, and then dumped into the river.

William Mitchell's death was never resolved and it registered as one of Maggie Lena's first and lasting encounters with tragedy. Mother and daughter felt each other's grief. As was customary, the neighbors shared what little they had. Even though William had held a fairly decent job for a black man in those times, the family still had no money or insurance. They were plunged into poverty. Her stepfather's death was a bitter lesson that would later play a major role in Maggie Lena's lifework.

Now Elizabeth Mitchell had to work harder than ever to support her two young children and to provide a home for her younger brothers. First, Frederick Draper, a laborer, came to live with her and the children. He stayed for two or three years, and then a younger brother, Edward, joined them. There was never enough money. Maggie's carefree days were over when she was barely ten. She had to assume the role of comforter and helpmate to her mother.

Their laundry work began early in the morning. They had to build a fire, draw water, and sort the clothes. Once the tubs were filled, they rubbed homemade lye soap onto the clothes and began the rhythmic task of rubbing them up and down, up and down, on the corrugated metal washboards. Their knuckles became sore from the strong soap and the scrubbing. Each piece of clothing had to be wrung out by hand. The constant twisting and wringing caused pain to shoot up Maggie's small arms and into her shoulders. Her back ached. Her only comfort was knowing that she was easing her mother's burden, and she longed for a time when they would not have to work so hard.

Elizabeth Mitchell's ironing work was highly recommended. She gave special attention to the fancy clothes with their finer fabrics and lace. The extreme heat of the stove used to heat the irons was almost unbearable, particularly on a summer's day. With sweat pouring from her brow, Elizabeth would often stop for a moment to wipe her face with an apron. Then she would resume the arduous task. She took pride in her work.

Maggie would help by folding the laundry. It smelled so fresh and clean. She carefully placed each item in the woven basket to be delivered to its owners. It was customary for black women to carry baskets on their heads. Maggie Walker would later remark, "*I was not born with a silver spoon in my mouth, but with a laundry basket practically on my head.*" Sometimes Johnnie would go with her. With Maggie holding her end up and little Johnnie holding his end down, they were a humorous sight as they carried the lopsided basket down the street. When Maggie was given a few pennies for delivering the laundry, she would save them; but sometimes she was given a biscuit with preserves, which she ate promptly.

❧ 5 ❧

Childhood Pranks

Early in the 1870s, the Richmond City Council, in a gesture of generosity rare at the time, established a system of segregated public education in Richmond. There were the schools opened for black children by the Freedman's Bureau also. Although Elizabeth Mitchell needed her daughter's help with the laundry, she knew it was far more important for Maggie Lena to get an education. This was no small task for a Southern black child.

Maggie went to the Lancaster School, which was named for John Lancaster, an English Quaker visionary who claimed he could teach literacy to the poor in only three months' time. This was called the first public school in Richmond because it accepted students regardless of their ability to pay tuition. More than likely, Maggie and her classmates knew what a privilege it was to go to school, but like most children they probably had fun, especially on the way. It was a time to frolic, tease, and chase each other.

Sometimes the children would lose track of time and have to run the rest of the way to get there before the bell rang. The walk to the school also carried them past the scary and mysterious jail and its prisoners. These were the subject of many strange tales that served as a constant reminder of what might happen to children if they misbehaved. Yet, like children of all times, their fear and fascination blended. Sometimes they would pass by the smelly, sweaty bodies of the Negro prisoners who were cramped in the jail. Or they would hear the pitiful singing of the men inside. Many of them had been imprisoned simply because of the Vagrancy Laws, or because they had no jobs or no family, or for some other petty offense for which a white man would not have been punished.

Another source of intrigue, on the hill above the jail was "Miss Lizzie," Elizabeth Van Lew. Once the war had ended, she had been ostracized by Richmonders, who accused her of being a Yankee spy. According to local legend, the Van Lew mansion had been part of the Underground

Railroad. It had a secret room that led to an underground tunnel. It was through this tunnel that many Union soldiers or runaway slaves had passed during the Civil War. Now the mistress of the big white house was known as "Crazy Bet" and she had very few friends. People said her only company was the forty cats she kept in her fast-decaying mansion. On one occasion, some boys had sneaked onto her property and tried to destroy some fruit trees. Miss Lizzie shocked them all by inviting the whole gang to an ice cream party! Years later, the Van Lew mansion—Maggie Lena's birthplace—was demolished to make way for the Bellevue School. Many people were saddened by the poor judgment exercised by the School Board because it destroyed one of Richmond's most beautiful landmarks. To this day, it is said that Crazy Bet's ghost haunts the school.

Besides her laundry duties and schoolwork, Maggie had the responsibility of caring for Johnnie, although she was only three years older. Johnnie was a handsome sprite. He had his mother's dark complexion. His brown eyes brimmed with laughter and mischief, and he

*Johnnie Mitchell, carefree and mischievous,
often frustrated his older sister Maggie.*

had an elfin charm. Maggie sometimes adored
and sometimes despised her brother, who had an
uncanny way of getting into trouble. Keeping up
with Johnnie took precious minutes she did not
have. He seemed to sense his sister's exasperation
and always found ways to make her job more dif-

21

ficult. Soon she realized that it was useless to try to keep up with him, but sometimes he and Maggie would venture into forbidden territory.

One of their favorite places of intrigue was Robinson's circus. Elizabeth had forbidden them to go because parents at that time were afraid that their children would be lured away from home to join the circus. But the circus drew them like a magnet. The fact that it was forbidden made it even more appealing to Maggie and Johnnie, so they ventured in to take a look. At first they watched from a distance. They were engrossed with the workers hurrying back and forth, setting up tents, and the performers practicing their acts and caring for the animals. They watched in silence and awe at all the activity. They saw expert aerialists, and of course, Louis, the famous horseback rider, who dazzled everybody by jumping on and off his running elk.

No one seemed to notice them, but their mother soon realized that they were missing from home. She called, "Maggie! Johnnie!" but there was no answer. They could not hear her for all the shouts and talk of the circus folk. It did not take long for Elizabeth to guess where her children had gone. She was furious! How many times

had she told them not to go to the circus lot?
She brushed her hair back, straightened her
apron, and walked briskly over to the tents. She
spotted them right away and did they ever get
scolded! Maggie was sorry that she had disobeyed
her mother, but Johnnie didn't seem to care.

❧ 6 ❧

"To Be Baptized . . ."

In the years of Reconstruction there was one thing, as constant as the North Star, which symbolized both freedom and stability for the black community. It was the black church. Initially, religion had been the slave owners' means for "soothing the savage African" to make him docile enough to accept slavery, but as time went on, the African-Americans created in the church an institution that suited their spiritual and cultural needs.

One church that had a prominent role in Richmond's politics was the First African Baptist Church. It had once been integrated and pastored by white men, although the white members of the congregation were leaving because of the increasing number of blacks and their fervent style of worship.

Gradually blacks assumed authority over

church matters. This authority spilled over into secular, or everyday, matters as well. Disputes were often settled by church elders before they were ever considered for outside intervention by the law. Political rallies had been held in the huge church, too. During these meetings men, women, and even children were allowed to speak their minds and vote on church issues. Dances and other social events were also held at church.

So when eleven-year-old Maggie Lena joined the First African Baptist Church during the Great Richmond Revival in 1878, a community and a tradition that would shape her life, it was more than a religious experience. She was also joining the largest black congregation in Richmond.

On the day of her baptism, Maggie arose especially early to prepare. She put on the long, white robe her mother had given her. She criss-crossed her braids atop her head, and pinned them with large hairpins. Then she covered her hair with a white cap. Elizabeth looked proudly at her daughter's image in the long mirror.

Together they walked the short distance to the First African Baptist Church and joined the other members for the baptismal procession. As they waited, parents gave last-minute instructions to their nervous children. When it was time to march down to the river, they marched and sang songs that mingled sweetly with the crisp stillness of the morning. Maggie stood on the banks of the James River in the early morning sun awaiting her turn to be baptized. She watched the ripples of water fan out from the baptismal spot as Reverend Holmes moved. He was poking around with a long wooden pole to check the depth of the water. He was dressed in a black cut-away suit and black rubber boots that came up to his hips. There in the pool, he reminded Maggie of a fisherman.

Her mind wandered back to the Sunday when she and Johnnie first stood beside the stone steps of the church. Brother and sister had watched the people in full Sunday display as they entered the building to worship: ladies and girls with fine frilly dresses, large fashionable hats, gloves, and dress shoes; men and boys with their hair slicked back, some wearing hats, looking dignified in their Sunday suits.

That day Deacon White had asked the Mitchell children to come in and join the others, but Maggie politely declined. Their clothes were not suitable. But, Maggie said, "I'll ask my mother if we can come next Sunday." When she tried to coax Johnnie a week later, he refused. He did not want to wear a silly old suit. Besides, the energetic Johnnie could not have sat still for two hours listening to a sermon.

Maggie woke up from her daydream. Now she was being guided gently into the water by Reverend Holmes. "I now baptize you in the name of the Father, the Son and the Holy Ghost . . ." He dipped her backwards into the river. As she emerged, the voices of the singers filled her ears and her spirit.

> "Take me to the water,
> Take me to the water,
> Take me to the water
> To be baptized . . ."

Maggie Lena's life of faith had begun.

❧ 7 ❧

Making Her Mark

Joining a fraternal organization during Maggie Lena Mitchell's time generated the same excitement as joining the basketball team, the cheering squad, or scouting does today. On her fourteenth birthday, July 15, 1881, Maggie joined the Good Idea Council #16 of the Independent Order of the Sons and Daughters of St. Luke. What a coincidence! Or was it? Throughout her life, she planned events on dates which had special meaning to her. Maggie had given herself a present which she could never forget. And, for the rest of her life, St. Luke would be as much a part of her as her birthday.

There were at least ten fraternal organizations, including the True Reformers and Daughters of Pythias, which she could have joined. She chose the Independent Order of St. Luke because the people whom she admired and respected most belonged to it: her mother, her Sunday School teacher, Mr. White, and Reverend Holmes.

Except for their secret rituals, fraternal organizations were set up very much like scout troops. Members earned badges and achieved rank when they learned specific rituals, performed mandatory tasks, and met the requirement for community service.

Maggie became a part-time volunteer. Her service gave her an insider's view of just how important St. Luke was to Richmond's black community. Members paid monthly dues to St. Luke and they received relief in the form of food, clothing, and counseling for employment. The dues also helped to pay burial expenses. The sick and shut-in would receive cards and visits from fellow members. The more she learned about the work of St. Luke, the more Maggie wanted to help. *Love, purity*, and *charity*, the values adopted by St. Luke, were eagerly embraced by Maggie. She rose quickly through the ranks of the organization, and was elected Secretary of the Good Idea Council at age sixteen.

As a teenager, Maggie Mitchell was also successfully juggling work at home, school, and volunteer work. Though St. Luke was important to her, maintaining a 75 percent average in her classes at the segregated Colored Normal School was even more important. She would not graduate if she fell below that average. Imagine how difficult it must have been to maintain an average of 75 percent in physiology, physics, chemistry, physical geography, astronomy, ancient history, algebra, geometry, rhetoric, penmanship, and language!

Maggie graduated in 1883, a year later than scheduled. The Richmond school board had added a foreign language to the requirements for graduation, and Maggie's class was delayed.

The graduating class of 1883 was an exceptional group of students. John Mitchell (no relation) would become editor, publisher, and owner of the *Richmond Planet* newspaper. Wendell Dabney would become editor of a newspaper in Cincinnati, Ohio. Mary Cary would become a medical doctor. Other members would be noted in education and law. And, of course, Maggie Lena Mitchell would become the first woman founder and president of a bank in America.

The decade from 1880 to 1890 was uncertain, and in many ways, the most turbulent time

*Maggie's high school graduation picture, 1883.
Her class organized the first school strike of
African-Americans to protest segregation.*

in Richmond, Virginia. Blacks became more and more vocal about segregation, about who should teach their children, and about the obvious inequalities between the education of black students and white students.

Maggie and her classmates certainly would have been aware of the debate. In their senior year, they exercised their rights as free Negro citizens by challenging an unacceptable school board policy. The long-standing policy required separate graduation ceremonies for Negro students. They held their graduation at a local church—usually First Baptist— because it had a seating capacity of about two thousand. White students held their graduation in the Richmond Theater. This policy would be toppled by the Class of 1883! The ten classmates boldly informed their principal, Miss Lizzie Knowles, that they would be graduating in the Richmond Theater along with the whites:

"Our class had a meeting and we were determined not to go to any church . . . The Richmond Theater or no where," wrote class spokesman, Wendell Dabney.

Called to a meeting with the faculty, principal, and school superintendent, the class was told that they should be satisfied with what they had because they were far better off than their ancestors. They were also threatened with not being allowed to graduate if they didn't go along with the program as outlined. But the gutsy ten stuck together.

"Our parents pay taxes just the same as you white folks, and you've got no business spending big money out of those taxes to pay for the theater for white children unless you do the same for black children," they fired back.

This was only the first battle. A second battle would have to be waged against the management of the Richmond Theater, which insisted on keeping its policy of segregation for Negroes and whites. Negroes would have to sit in the balcony and whites in the orchestra seats. Maggie's class angrily refused:

"We don't want the Theater unless it is granted to us as it is granted to others," they responded.

There was just not enough room in the balcony to accommodate the many family members and friends who wanted to attend the graduation. What an insult it would be for their mothers, fathers, sisters, and brothers to have to sit in what was called "the peanut gallery." Scared yet determined, the Class of 1883 decided to boycott. They wouldn't use the church or the theater! Instead, they chose to hold their graduation in the assembly room of the Normal School. The space was inadequate, but they had made their point. The Class of 1883 went down in history as the organizers of the first school strike of blacks in America!

Just at this time, when Maggie was on the brink of womanhood, the father she had never known, Eccles Cuthbert, entered her life again. He had purchased a graduation dress for her, but Elizabeth Mitchell severely rebuked him and threw the dress away. How dare he try to intrude on them now! Years later Maggie reflected on the hardship of her birth, and her mother's growing determination to raise her daughter:

"The thought of my . . . birth, my mother, humble ignorant girl who brought me into life, her early struggle to hide me, her gain in courage to acknowledge me as

her own when my father wanted to take me from her, and place me in a Catholic School in Baltimore. . . . My mother's love for me coming to the surface made her the mother of a girl who needed [love?]."

❧ 8 ❧

The Young Teacher

During the unrest of the 1880s, the church became the primary arena for political activism, and the pulpit was effectively used to rally support for the concerns of black citizens. On May 22, 1882, a group of Negro leaders gathered at First African Baptist Church to address the most important issues. The room was charged with energy as they brainstormed and discussed them. The hottest topic on the floor was who should teach their children, Negro teachers or white teachers? Among the most vocal opponents of white schoolmarms teaching Negro children was Attorney E. A. Randolph. He believed that white teachers could not possibly have the same feeling for their Negro students as a Negro teacher could. White teachers didn't live in the community, and they didn't associate with their students other than at school.

"[They don't] greet them in the Sunday schools and churches, walk with them upon the streets, and in many other ways win their entire confidence as all teachers should," he said.

Negroes also argued that the Normal School training which Negro teachers received was meaningless unless they could find jobs as teachers, and they believed that white teachers were taking the jobs which qualified black teachers should have.

Finally, the Richmond school board gave in to the mounting pressure from the black community. In the fall of 1883, they decided to hire black teachers for the Negro schools. The only exception was the Normal School, which continued to be staffed by a white principal and white teachers.

Maggie Mitchell was one of the fortunate few to be hired to teach that year. She was offered a teaching position by her former teacher and principal, Miss Lizzie Knowles. Maggie accepted the job at a salary of $35 per month, and was assigned to Valley School, where James H. Hayes was principal. She taught First Primary B (the second semester of first grade) for half of the year, and third Grammar B (second semester of third grade) the second half. During her third and final year of teaching, Maggie Mitchell taught Third Grammar A, and earned $42.50 a month. She was moving up the career ladder.

Schools for Negroes in Richmond, including Valley School, were very poorly kept. The school board never seemed to have enough money to repair or maintain the buildings. Instead, the money was funneled into building new schools for white students, and in keeping their existing schools in top condition. Consequently, when Maggie Mitchell opened the door to her classroom on her first day as a teacher, she was greeted by the same pitiful conditions that had existed when she was a student at Lancaster: the large, cracked blackboard, ashy with age; dilapidated desks arranged like tombstones; and tattered textbooks that had been handed down from the white students. She sighed. There was still a long way to go.

As a teacher, Maggie Lena Mitchell had become one of the black elite in Richmond. Teachers had a great deal of influence in the community because they symbolized education, the main thing that could help their people escape from poverty. As a member of this privileged group, Maggie came in close contact with prominent men and women of Richmond such as the Yale-trained Attorney Randolph, publisher and businessman R. T. Hill, her principal, James Hayes, and Rosa Dixon Bowser, an activist. Mrs. Bowser was the first Negro woman teacher in Richmond, and a graduate of the first Normal School class in 1872. Maggie admired Rosa Bowser's pioneering spirit, and the way she accomplished whatever was necessary to meet the needs of people. She had founded the Women's League to raise money for the defense of two Negro women who were wrongly accused of murdering their employer; she had started a night school for men and boys; and she was the first president of the Virginia Teachers' Association.

Maggie Mitchell was very active in such groups, the Women's Missionary and Educational Society of Virginia and the Acme Literary Association among them. Like ripples on still water, the influence of Negro women educators radiated into the community, changing the lives of their black sisters and brothers. Drawing on their collective strengths and their common bond as women, they organized to uplift themselves and their people.

✠ 9 ✠

Family Matters

According to the statutes of Virginia, Maggie Mitchell could not teach after marriage. No woman could. Therefore, her three-year teaching career formally ended with her marriage to Armstead Walker on September 14, 1886. Maggie obviously enjoyed teaching, for even after this, she continued to teach at St. Luke, in Sunday School, and on the streets of Richmond. She could have gone back to teaching after Armstead's death in 1915. By then, she was too deeply involved with St. Luke and the Penny Savings Bank.

Like so many other couples of the period, Maggie and Armstead met at one of the numerous church-sponsored activities for youth. Church was *the* place in Richmond to meet and socialize. Maggie and Armstead could also have been introduced by Armstead's sister Emma

Maggie and Armstead Walker. The teacher and the handsome young contractor met on the steps of the First African Baptist Church, a social center for Richmond Negroes. They married September 14, 1886.

Walker, who taught with Maggie at Valley School. But, according to Maggie's official biographer, Wendell Dabney, the two met at a favorite gathering place, the steps of First African Baptist Church. Armstead was a good catch. He was an 1875 graduate of the Colored Normal School; he was handsome; and he worked with his father in the family's brick contracting business. The Walkers had built some of the finest brick homes in Richmond, Virginia.

For a short while, Maggie and Armstead lived with his parents on North Seventh Street, but by 1888, they had moved into their own home at 719 North Third Street. Marriage may have ended Maggie's teaching career, but it did not keep this energetic lady from working. She began to devote more and more time to helping at St. Luke. She also remained active in the teachers' association which held discussion forums on Monday evenings, the literary club, and other service organizations which kept her connected with her community.

But family was also important, and Maggie was eager to have a baby. Her firstborn came into life with a wretched struggle on December 9,

1890. The entry in her diary on December 9, 1925, describes his birth:

> *"His birth was unnatural in that he had to be taken [with forceps] by Drs. Ross, Michaux, and Dismond. He was crushed about the face and head. We named him Russell Eccles Talmage Walker. I was ill, but happy. I was so anxious for a little baby—to love, to rear, to follow by day and night, to see develop into a great and useful man. . . . [But] the little baby was placed on the hearth to die, so bruised was he."*

Russell's survival was a miracle in 1890, particularly when most babies were born at home, and before the age of life-saving devices such as respirators, or incubators, or neonatal [newborn] departments in hospitals. But Russell did not die. Careful nursing brought him around. The Eccles part of his name may have been in tribute to his grandfather, who was still in Richmond at the time. He would leave the city that same year.

"For five months I was confined to bed and house, and during that time the baby Russell grew," Maggie later wrote.

In 1893, Maggie and Armstead had another son whom they named Armstead Mitchell. He was born on July 8, and was given his father's first name and his mother's maiden name. Armstead Mitchell Walker lived just seven months. He died on February 4, 1894 and his death was a terrible blow to Armstead and Maggie. They were grateful that Russell had survived.

During the same year, Maggie's brother Johnnie returned home from New York, sick and penniless. In a way, he had been her first child. She loved and protected him, and she adored his humor, generosity, and carefree nature. All of her efforts to nurse him back to good health failed. Johnnie died on April 23, 1894 of tuberculosis. Less than three months after her little Armstead's death, Maggie was grieving again.

Another child, Margaret Anderson, would soon fill some of the emptiness in the Walkers' hearts. Polly, as she was affectionately called, moved into the Walker home in 1895. She was Armstead's niece, his sister's child. Armstead and Maggie apparently adopted her, for she was always referred to, even in the census records, as their adopted child. At any rate, Polly was a de-

*Maggie and sons Russell (left)
and Melvin (right).*

voted daughter and spent most of her life caring
for the family.

In 1894, Maggie and Armstead moved again,
this time to a home across the street from Armstead's parents. Melvin DeWitt was born in their
new home at 907 North Seventh Street on August 10, 1897. They were thankful that his birth
was uneventful and without problems.

Melvin was carefree, very much like his

Uncle Johnnie had been. He would often sneak away to play with the boys at their secret gathering place under the James River bridge in Shockoe Valley. It was not a safe place for children to play, and his parents certainly would not have approved. But Melvin loved courting danger.

Maggie and Armstead spoiled Russell and Melvin and made no secret about it. However, being spoiled did not mean that they were excused from practicing their parents' values of thrift, respect, and responsibility. The boys had chores to do in order to get an allowance, part of which had to be saved. Russell and Melvin were also required to go to church, whether they wanted to or not. In the Walker family, church was as important as education and work.

❧ 10 ❧

St. Luke

By 1895, Maggie Walker had dug her heels in the sand and was aggressively learning the business of St. Luke. The former teacher's love for children motivated her to push for the establishment of a juvenile branch of the Independent Order of St. Luke. She diligently pursued this idea at the 1895 convention in Norfolk, Virginia, for she believed a juvenile branch would make the Order more competitive with its rival, the True Reformers.

The push for change was on. Maggie agreed to chair a committee to draft the laws, rules, and regulations for a juvenile division, and to report to the Grand Council at the very same meeting. Speculation was that she and her committee either had the draft ready or they worked extremely fast to put one together. *"Our hope for the future lies with the children—the youth of our race,"* Mrs. Walker urged in her address, and she convinced St. Luke to establish a juvenile branch immediately. Within a year, it had mushroomed to a thousand members! Two years later, Maggie Walker was made Grand Deputy Matron of the Juvenile Branch, a title she cherished and one which she literally took to her grave. It is inscribed on her headstone.

With the help of other able and dedicated Matrons, the Juvenile Department provided opportunities for children to learn and to have fun. Two slogans framed their ideals: "As a twig is bent, so it grows," and "Suffer little children to come unto me," and each child knew the meaning of them. Circles were made up of smaller groups within the Juvenile Branch, and were given the names of flowers such as violet, sunflower, marigold, and daisy. To encourage attendance, Maggie Walker suggested prizes to reward children who came to each meeting from September through July. The grand prize was an autographed copy of Mrs. Walker's photograph!

The unsuspecting children didn't know that they were being groomed educationally and socially, but they were. The Matrons were trained to cultivate the very best in them, and to plan

The Juvenile Branch of St. Luke used parades, storytelling, and talent shows to teach children the importance of self-help and community involvement.

each month's activities to insure it. Children were polished in the social graces, and were taught the importance of self-help and community involvement. Their religious training and the value of thrift were emphasized. But all this was disguised in the backyard parties, talent shows, storytelling, and parades that Maggie helped to organize. She knew that children would respond to fun events.

Each year around Thanksgiving, St. Luke sponsored Sunshine Day. It was a day to celebrate community and to encourage members to do something for others who were less fortunate. They were asked to send out a "ray of sunshine" by visiting the sick, running errands, or taking food to a needy family. Circle members also enjoyed the annual parade, for this was the chance they got to show off to their communities. And, show off they did. Wearing their finest Sunday clothes and sashes laden with badges which they had earned during the year, they strutted through the neighborhood as proud as Springtime showing its new flowers.

In 1899, the Independent Order of St. Luke held its thirty-second annual convention in Hinton, West Virginia. This was perhaps the most crucial meeting that Maggie would attend; the fate of the "Grand Old Order" was hanging in the balance. It was losing members, and fewer members meant less money to pay claims. Some members felt that St. Luke had outlived its usefulness. Other members believed that it was in such bad shape because of poor financial management. Feelings ran high on both sides.

Maggie had taken the train to Hinton. In

those days, trains and horses and wagons were the main sources of transportation. As the locomotive chugged through the Blue Ridge Mountains, Maggie admired the lush green trees and shrubs, and the occasional patches of brightly colored flowers which sprouted among the jagged rocks. It reminded her of her mother's patchwork quilts, each piece sewn in just the right place, creating a lovely design.

When she arrived at the convention, she noticed people gathered in small groups, and she overheard them talking about the fate of St. Luke. It was even rumored that the Grand Secretary, William Forrester, was going to resign.

William Forrester opened the annual meeting by explaining why St. Luke was failing. He had worked hard to keep it going, but he wasn't getting the cooperation he needed. Members were losing interest. Then he went really way out on a limb and suggested that maybe St. Luke had served its purpose and should cease operation. He ended by announcing his resignation as Right Worthy Grand Secretary. Sitting there, Maggie thought about her own stepfather, William Mitchell, and how he had died without insurance to help pay for his burial, or to help her mother with her and Johnnie. Her father's death had taught her that people need the kind of help that St. Luke provided.

The official records showed the true picture. The number of councils had dropped to fifty-seven, and adult membership had dwindled to just over a thousand, fewer than the number in the newly-created Juvenile Branch. Only $31.61 was left in the treasury, with outstanding debts of $400. Amidst a lot of bickering and heated discussion, the election of new officers was held. The final choice was made. Maggie Lena Walker emerged as the new Right Worthy Grand Secretary of the Independent Order of St. Luke!

In typical fashion, Maggie got right to work. Her first two official decisions showed that take-charge attitude for which she became so well-known. To help stop the financial drain on St. Luke, she reduced her salary to $100 a month, one-third the $300 salary of the previous Grand Secretary. Her next decision was to bring the operations of St. Luke under one roof. On August 15, 1899, Maggie Lena Walker was on her way to becoming a nationally recognized black business-woman and leader.

During that first year of reviving St. Luke,

she traveled frequently to Maryland, New Jersey, and New York, where she gave pep talks, encouraged new people to join, and invited former members to return. Maggie Walker wrote the councils she could not visit, and her message was the same: Grow, grow, grow!

With Maggie Lena Walker as its chief executive officer, St. Luke was booming. Membership increased dramatically. But Maggie wanted the Order to be more than a beneficial society that paid sick and death claims. She foresaw a large business enterprise operating out of the grand four-story brick building on St. James Street, and she used her annual report to pass her vision on to the members. Maggie Walker addressed the 1901 convention with the zeal of a prophet:

> "Eternal vigilance is the price of success. . . . Brethren and sisters, we need to start and operate a factory for the making of clothing for women and children, men's underwear and a millinery store. We have the means, the brains; we are simply waiting for the motion to be made, seconded, put and carried, and our Order will take a new lease of life."

St. Luke was enjoying new life mainly because of Maggie Walker's ability to see possibilities and potential. Her insight wasn't just confined to the Order either. She saw potential in people. She frequently talked about people she had helped through St. Luke.

One of her favorite stories was about a boot-black [shoeshine man]. When she first met this struggling entrepreneur, he was working in all kinds of weather out on the sidewalk at the corner of Second and Clay streets. He couldn't afford to rent a building or even a space in a building. He joined St. Luke, and was taught how to save and manage his money. Once he had accumulated fifty dollars, Maggie Walker helped him find a place to rent. He located a little place with three chairs, and his shoeshine business prospered. In seven years, he owned a shop with twelve chairs. He bought a home for his mother for $1,900 and paid cash to furnish it. His bank account never fell below five hundred dollars.

In Maggie Walker's mind, education was truly the key to success. She believed that St. Luke needed to be involved in helping young people get an education beyond high school. So, she proposed to the Grand Council that an educational loan fund be established to aid students who wanted to go to college. She knew firsthand that many capable students could not afford to go to college. Their parents simply did not have the money. The educational loan fund would assist those youngsters by allowing their parents to borrow money for tuition.

The *St. Luke Herald* was another of Maggie's ideas. *"What we need is an organ: a newspaper to herald and proclaim the work of our Order. No business, no enterprise, which has to deal with the public, can be pushed successfully without a newspaper,"* she stated. A special section of the *Herald* was devoted to the poems, stories, and articles which St. Luke children wrote. You can imagine the thrill children felt receiving the paper with their work published in it!

Maggie Walker spent several years learning the insurance business from the powerful and astute businessmen at Southern Aid Insurance Company. Southern Aid had been established in 1893 to provide employment for Normal School graduates, to give these graduates a chance to use their academic skills instead of doing menial work. Southern Aid was the first insurance company owned and operated by blacks which was not connected to a beneficial society. It was also the largest Negro-owned and operated insurance company in the country.

Up to this time, white insurance companies had had a monopoly on the insurance market. Maggie Walker's new enterprises placed St. Luke in direct competition with white-owned businesses, for both were competing for the same dollars from the black population.

By 1903, St. Luke had become a business conglomerate employing hundreds of people and meeting all aspects of the business needs of its members and the community: insurance, newspaper, clothing store, printing press, and educational loans.

❧ 11 ❧

Fighting Jim Crow

The turn of the century was an ugly time in the history of Richmond as the "black codes" were enacted all over the South. These were laws enacted by states and cities which allowed the segregation of blacks and whites. They were used by the white majority to restrict and disenfranchise the Negro people, and they wiped out most of the progress blacks had made since the Civil War.

The black codes, better known as "Jim Crow" laws, grew as rampantly as the kudzu vine. Like the fast-growing plant, these political "kudzus" strangled all the accomplishments Negroes had made.

As soon as blacks would get a toe in the door of the Southern economy, two or three other doors would slam shut. Negroes were disqualified from construction work on City Hall and other city jobs, because of their race and because they were members of the Republican party. Southern whites increasingly felt that the Republican party did not speak for them.

To make matters worse, the *Dispatch*, the white newspaper, frequently ran disparaging articles about blacks to make them seem ignorant and inferior through so-called news and caricature. To counter-attack, such Negro papers as the *Richmond Planet* had the courage to crusade on behalf of blacks. The *St. Luke Herald* also joined this crusade for justice: *"It [the Herald] is of the people, by the people, and for the people. It is the people's organ, the people's paper, devoted to their every interest, the champion of their rights,"* Mrs. Walker stated.

The right to vote was being stolen from blacks by literacy tests which would have required the Ph.D. in history to pass; poll taxes; and other laws. Even well-educated blacks had severe restrictions placed upon them. They could only serve or administer to other blacks and usually for far less pay than their white counterparts. Many of these business and professional people had to supplement their incomes with various and sometimes menial jobs.

It seemed that the more restrictions which were imposed on blacks in Richmond, the stronger the people became as they continued to chop away at the kudzu vines of social injustice. If any benefit can be found in the black codes, it would be that they forced the black community to unite. Women's groups, fraternal organizations, colleges, and black-owned newspapers organized to challenge them. In 1901, Maggie Walker wrote:

> *"It [the Herald] comes to cry aloud in thunder tones against proscription, against injustice, against mob-law, against "Jim Crow" Cars, against the curtailment of Public School privileges, and against the enactment and enforcement of laws which place a premium upon white illiteracy, and treat black illiteracy as a crime."*

Maggie Walker and other black leaders sought solutions to their common problems, because Jim Crow laws affected every conceivable aspect of Negro life: church, employment, home, education, insurance, and even death and burial. Finding ways to fight these laws became the topic of discussion at national Negro conferences at

Atlanta University in Atlanta, Georgia; Hampton Institute in Hampton, Virginia, and other places.

Nonetheless, all eyes were on Richmond on April 1, 1904. It was official. Beginning on April 20, Virginia Passenger & Power Company was going to enforce the segregated streetcar law. The announcement made front-page news.

TO SEPARATE RACES IN CARS:

P & P to Post Notices
in Conformance with the New Law

Then the details of the law were given, and the notice which would be posted in the streetcars was printed. It stated in part:

> The conductor of this car is authorized by law to separate white and colored passengers and to designate the portions of this car, or the seats therein, which may be occupied by white passengers and which may be occupied by colored passengers, and to change such designation from time to time, and to require any passenger to change his or her seat when and as often as he may deem necessary and proper.

Virginia had also passed a law which empowered conductors and motormen to enforce the law as they saw fit. They were even allowed to carry and use guns:

> Any person failing or refusing to obey the direction of the conductor is liable for a fine of $25, and may be also ejected from the car for such refusal. The conductor or motorman of this car are made by law special policemen while on duty.

Accepting the humiliation of having to sit in the rear of the trolley and moving as often as the conductor instructed was one thing, but encountering gun-packing conductors and motormen was another. It was this last issue which sounded the alarm among Negroes that their status as citizens of Richmond had truly worsened. At the same time, it ignited a spirit of resistance unlike anything Richmond had witnessed before. In the beginning, black protest took the form of resolutions, mass meetings, and editorials in newspapers. John Mitchell, Jr., editor of the *Richmond Planet*, wrote, "We shall agitate and agitate. We shall never willingly submit."

However, the two most effective means of resistance were out-and-out refusal to comply and the streetcar boycott.

SHE WANTED AIR,
BUT IT COST $10:

Negro Fined for Disregarding Jim Crow Law
on Trolley Car

declared a July 11, 1904, article in the *News Leader*:

> "Back seat, please," ordered Conductor R. A. Fleshman.
>
> "I ain't a-gwine to do it," replied Laura Smith.

According to the paper, Laura Smith had taken the trolley downtown without incident. On her return trip, she sat in the same seat by the window which she had occupied before. All she wanted was air— "the kind furnished by the open window of the seat from which the conductor sought to eject her," the paper reported. When Laura Smith reached a transfer point, the conductor turned her over to the police. She was fined $10.

THE NEGROES WILL WALK

read the *Richmond Times Dispatch* headline the day after a mass meeting at the True Reformers'

Hall on April 19, 1904. More than six hundred blacks met to show their solidarity, and to speak out against the Jim Crow law. Present at the meeting were five bank officials, four physicians, five insurance executives, two officials of benevolent organizations, one college president, a professor, one attorney, and three funeral directors. In speech after speech, they vowed to walk rather than conform.

"Don't argue the question; don't get into controversy. Don't say anything, but walk," advised Patsie Anderson, manager of the Women's Union Grocery Company and the only woman speaker at the mass meeting.

"We don't want guns, we want peace, and the way to keep it is to let the white people have their cars. I entreat you to stay off the cars," thundered news editor John Mitchell, Jr.

"The very dangerous power placed in the hands of hotheaded and domineering white men . . . will certainly provoke trouble, when they order Negroes to this seat or that, to move from seat to seat at their sweet will," cautioned the *St. Luke Herald*.

The streetcar boycott lasted about six months. During that time, walking became the principal means of transportation for Richmond's blacks. A few Negro businesses, especially funeral directors and delivery men, provided free transportation. The five black bank presidents proposed setting up a fund to finance a black transit company to replace Virginia Passenger & Power.

Was the 1904 streetcar boycott a success? The white newspapers said no, that only a small percentage of Negroes were walking. The black press said yes. As many as "eighty to ninety percent of the local Negroes were participating in the boycott," the *Planet* reported. By the end of the year, Virginia Passenger & Power had gone bankrupt.

It would take another sixty years to regain some political control in Richmond, but the children of slaves were still able somehow to develop the means of creative self-expression and survival. Their institutions—churches, fraternal and mutual aid societies, businesses, newspapers, and literary clubs—became the bricks and mortar of black survival during this dramatic period. An amazing thing is that in spite of all the roadblocks they encountered, 43 percent of Negroes had become literate, according to the 1890 U. S.

Census. This is remarkable for a people who had been free for only thirty years.

But while blacks were making progress there were still forces working against them. The political "kudzu" of Jim Crow was used to maintain white supremacy. Its roots were deep. It would not be until the Civil Rights era, also known as the "Second Reconstruction," that blacks would truly be enfranchised, and only then after arduous struggle.

⸎ 12 ⸎

Pennies to Dollars

It was against this landscape of oppression that Negroes continued to establish businesses in Jackson Ward. Banks, mom-and-pop stores, insurance companies, millinery shops, barber shops, and funeral homes flourished. Determined to be self-sufficient, Negroes had banded together to provide for their own needs.

This determination and sense of camaraderie undergirded the establishment of St. Luke Penny Savings Bank. Believing that people could "turn nickels into dollars" by pooling their money and lending it out, at interest, Maggie Walker crusaded for the establishment of a bank, owned and operated by St. Luke. It was by far the best idea that the thirty-six-year-old Maggie Lena Walker had conceived. "*Let us put our money together; let us use our monies; let us put our money to usury [interest] among ourselves and reap the benefits our-*

*Negro-owned businesses such as these had a
chance to prosper because the business
conglomerate of St. Luke met many aspects of the
black community's needs.*

selves," Maggie told the delegation at the 1901 convention.

It was well into the fall and there were a few leaves lingering on the trees. The rest had been taken prisoner by the wind. The November air was brisk and invigorating. Maggie was grateful for the coolness as she rushed from one place to another in preparation for the opening of St. Luke Penny Savings Bank. There were many last-minute details which she could not trust to anyone else. For one thing, she had to consider the responses she would make to the newspaper reporters. She knew that the opening of St. Luke Penny Savings Bank would be covered in the press since she, as president and founder, was a black woman.

Maggie anxiously prepared herself and her family for the big day. It went far better than she had hoped. People came from as far away as New York to make deposits in the new bank, and there was a steady stream of people all day and until about eleven o'clock at night.

A local newspaper reported that "the main office has been crowded all day with colored people representing all stations of Afro-American Society." This was an historic day in Richmond,

Virginia. Total receipts for the first day were
$9,430.44! That was a lot of money in those
days. The pennies that Mrs. Walker encouraged
people to save had mounted. Imagine 943,044
pennies! In the early 1900s a penny was valuable.

Why, with a penny you could buy a small
bag of assorted candy, or a large lollipop, or three
"johnny cake" cookies, or five jawbreakers. A
bottle of Pepsi Cola cost 5¢. Or you could buy a
pound of gingersnaps for 4¢. A little boy could
buy a cap for 19¢ or a double-breasted wool suit
for $2.50. And a leather belt cost only 25¢.
Imagine that! A penny was valuable, especially
for struggling people. So they took their pennies
to the bank to open savings accounts. Maggie's
dream of a bank, owned and operated by blacks,
became a reality on November 2, 1903.

Children were also savers! Each child was
given a small cardboard "rainy day" bank in
which to put pennies. As soon as their banks
were filled with pennies, they would take them
to the Penny Savings Bank to be counted and
deposited into their very own bank accounts.

*"Numbers of our children have bank accounts
of from one hundred to four hundred dollars. They
sell papers, cut grass, do chores, run errands and*

work in stores on Saturdays. We teach them to save with a definite purpose," Maggie Walker said.

Some children also opened Christmas savings accounts with a penny and paid a penny or a nickel each week. By Christmas, they had saved enough money to buy each member of their family a present.

Maggie Walker had a knack for managing people and money. She was always on the alert for newer or improved ways of doing business, and had begun using the new accounting system at Penny Savings which her son Russell had suggested.

A law passed in Virginia in July 1910, requiring all state banks to be inspected annually by the Virginia Corporation Commission. From this time on, black banks were being held under a microscope by state bank examiners who were looking for the smallest violation of the banking codes. The first target of the Commission was the True Reformers' Bank, the oldest and largest black bank in Richmond. The Commission found that too much of True Reformers' money was tied up in mortgages and loans. They felt this would severely limit True Reformers' ability to pay out money for death claims, so they suspended the bank's license.

The True Reformers had no alternative but to petition for receivership. (Receivership occurs when a bank no longer has money to do business, and the state takes it over). The True Reformers' Bank closed on October 25, 1910. When it failed, a shock wave went throughout the black community, especially other Negro banks. If True Reformers' could fail, others would certainly be doomed to the same fate.

St. Luke Penny Savings was not spared the scrutiny of the examiners. It underwent an extensive audit on November 10, 1910. Fortunately, the board of directors of Penny Savings Bank had made excellent business decisions, and had kept excellent records. The success of this first inspection can also be attributed to Russell Walker's accounting procedure. Russell had taken correspondence courses through Loyola University to learn a new bookkeeping system which he had used at the bank. The Penny Savings Bank was finally declared okay.

Another law enacted in November 1910 required banks to separate from fraternal organizations. Thus, St. Luke Penny Savings Bank was forced to cut its ties with St. Luke. There was tremendous fallout from this new law. With each new restriction, the black banking community was getting smaller. The two black banks which survived all the new regulations were John Mitchell's Mechanics Bank and St. Luke Penny Savings.

You can imagine the pride St. Luke members felt at having come through all of the new banking regulations with a clear record. Their survival depended a great deal upon the management style of Maggie Walker, who chose the most qualified people to work at the bank. She also spent long tiring hours herself working to make sure the bank succeeded.

On October 31, 1911, less than a year after the bank examination, the Penny Savings Bank had moved into a new three-story building designed especially for them by a black architect named Charles A. Russell. Located at First and Marshall streets, the new bank was a tremendous source of pride. It had large windows on the first floor, brass grills at the tellers' cages, and mahogany furniture in Mrs. Walker's office.

Mrs. Walker often stood near the front door

St. Luke Penny Savings Bank, later the
Consolidated Bank and Trust Company of
Richmond, with Maggie Walker at the window.
Note her portrait on the wall to the left.

behind the tellers to greet each customer with a
warm smile. She was clearly the chief executive
officer of St. Luke Penny Savings Bank. The deposits in St. Luke Bank increased 300 percent
from 1910 to 1920. Deposits had grown from
$103,293 in 1911, to $376,288 in 1919. In keeping with the expanded services the bank now of-

fered, the name was changed to St. Luke Bank and Trust Company.

Nonetheless, the three remaining black banks, St. Luke Bank and Trust, Second Street Savings Bank, and Commercial Bank and Trust were experiencing a decline in deposits caused by more stringent banking regulations and other economic factors that would ultimately lead to the stock market crash of 1929. They knew that this was going to cause one or all of them to fail, so they agreed that the consolidation of their assets would be in the best interest of all. After several meetings, Commercial pulled out of the merger discussion, but St. Luke and Second Street decided to make a new bank "with a larger capital reserve fund and more uniform management." Consolidated Bank and Trust opened for business on January 2, 1930.

Today, the main branch of Consolidated Bank and Trust Company is located at First and Marshall streets in Richmond, diagonally across from the original site. Run by Maggie Walker until her death in 1934, Consolidated Bank and Trust Company is the oldest continuously operating black bank in America!

❧ 13 ❧

Tragedy Strikes Again

Back in 1905, the Walkers had purchased a home at 110½ East Leigh Street. It was in the Jackson Ward neighborhood known as "Society Row." High society blacks such as doctors, lawyers, and business leaders lived there. The Walkers' two-story brick dwelling was very close to houses on either side of it, and it was deeper than it was wide. As the family grew, so did the house. The twenty-five room mansion was exquisitely decorated with beautifully designed wallpaper, rich mahogany furniture, and crystal lamps. Potted plants were everywhere. Large gold-leafed mirrors hung in the parlor, and the library shelves were filled with the classics, encyclopedias, and books such as *A History of the American Negro*, and *The Ambitious Woman in Business*. Besides containing the best in literature, the library

*Now a National Historic Site of the United States
National Park Service, the richly-appointed
Walker house on East Leigh Street was a gathering
place for such influential people as Booker T.
Washington and Mary McCleod Bethune.*

served as a gallery of famous people with whom Mrs. Walker associated.

People were always visiting the Walker home. Some would drop by to say hello or to reveal the latest gossip. Others attended the many dinners, parties, or meetings that were held there. Maggie Walker entertained many dignitaries. Among the most noted were Booker T. Washington, founder of Tuskegee Institute; Janie Porter Barrett, founder of the Industrial School for Colored Girls and winner of a Spingarn Medal for community work; and Mary McCleod Bethune, founder of Bethune Cookman College.

By 1915, and in spite of the Jim Crow laws, the Walker family was doing well. Melvin had completed his third year at Shaw University in Raleigh, North Carolina, and was having a good time. Russell, then twenty-five years old, had a promising career at Penny Savings Bank. Armstead's business was successful. Maggie was at the zenith of her career. Then suddenly something happened! It was as though a tidal wave had come and swept up Maggie, her family, and the whole community.

It was a hot, sultry June day. Russell had seen some prowlers climb the ladder to the roof of the

Walker house. He told his father. They called the police, who gave a very casual inspection of the roof. Seeing nothing there, they told the family to call them if there was any further problem. The Walkers remained uneasy.

Armstead borrowed a gun from a neighbor. Later in the evening when Maggie, Polly, and Russell were sitting on the porch seeking relief from the stifling heat, a neighbor sent her son to report that they had seen a man wandering on the roof. As soon as the boy brought the news, Russell rushed up to his father's room and got the pistol. He crouched in the doorway of the lavatory and fired through the bamboo sunscreen at the end of the porch. He yelled to his mother, "I got him, I got him!" Maggie rushed to the scene, and when she saw who Russell had shot, she screamed. Russell came closer. "My God, it is Pappa!" he groaned as he collapsed against the wall.

Armstead was pronounced dead by the coroner, who declared the shooting accidental. Nonetheless, Russell was drawn into a vicious whirlpool of rumor and speculation. Newspapers carried such headlines as "THE KILLING OF

ARMSTEAD WALKER," and people began saying that the shooting was not an accident. Armstead's body was taken from the grave to be reexamined. Finally, Russell was arrested and put on trial for the murder of his father! For five long, turbulent months, trial dates were set and postponed.

Finally on November 12, the case was called. All day Saturday the witnesses from both sides were heard. *"I, subjected to a most rigid examination, was in the chair for over three hours,"* Maggie recalled painfully. *"At 10 o'clock Saturday night, the court adjourned until Monday. My son was carried to jail to spend that time. I hated awfully to see him go."* Maggie went home and prayed! At 10:00 Monday morning, she returned to the courtroom to hear the jury's verdict.

"When the jurors returned, a death-like silence filled the courtroom," Maggie later wrote in her diary. But the verdict was in.

"Not guilty!" the foreman reported. Maggie swept Russell into her loving arms. At least her son had been saved. They returned to the emptiness and sadness of their home, determined to pick up the pieces and renew their lives. The or-

deal had left Maggie feeling like a ship on a deso-
late sea. She had lost her husband and had
almost lost her son, again.

Yet her relief was temporary. Just when it
seemed like the streak of bad luck was over, another problem loomed ahead. The circumstances
surrounding Armstead's death created bitter feelings among a few St. Luke members. Maggie
Walker's enemies sought to use the tragedy as a
reason to remove her from office. The matter was
brought up at the next general meeting. Members of the Grand Council filled the huge auditorium of St. Luke. Maggie's leadership was on
trial. Her accusers pretended to care very deeply
for her and to show their appreciation for all she
had done; but they felt St. Luke had been scan-
dalized by the recent events. They demanded her
resignation from the position of Grand Secretary.

"*They told in well chosen words of the demand
for new leadership, [and] dwelt upon the notoriety
brought upon the great organization as a result of the
happenings in the home of the Grand Secretary,*" she
wrote.

Still weakened and saddened by the tragedy,
Maggie somehow summoned the strength to

fight back. When she stood up to face the people she thought were her friends, there was a cloud of suspense in the auditorium. No one knew what she would say. Then she spoke. She reminded them of her dedication, her hard work, and the progress that had been made under her leadership. And, in her most eloquent and persuasive manner, she convinced even her accusers that she was willing and able to continue to work on behalf of the Independent Order of St. Luke. Cheers and applause broke out and Maggie received a standing ovation. She had overcome yet another obstacle and would remain Grand Secretary for nineteen more years.

⊰ 14 ⊱

Woman of Action

Nothing disturbed Maggie Walker more than people who sat around talking about a problem and doing nothing to help solve it. She compared them to the fig tree in the Bible. They looked good, but they weren't bearing any fruit.

"Jesus cursed the fig tree because it was a LIVING LIE! It stood there, by the wayside, in the sight of all the world, claiming by its appearance that it was fruitful; for upon the fig tree FRUIT comes once and then [come] leaves. But, when the test was made—there was nothing—nothing but leaves," she once told an audience in Washington, D.C.

She spent the better part of her adult life campaigning on behalf of women. Her most passionate speeches were about the condition of women, and her commitment to their uplift.

"Whatever I have done in this life has been because I love women. Love to be surrounded by them.

Love to hear them all talk at once. Love to listen to their trials and troubles. Love to help them," she reassured a group of women.

Her speeches were more than idle words. The women who worked for her had respectable jobs and decent wages. She encouraged them to get practical job training and a good education. She observed and rewarded highly motivated workers at St. Luke. As an inspirational and motivational speaker she used examples of real people who had worked steadily toward a goal—usually the goal of financial independence.

"When any of our girls are advanced to making as much as fifty dollars a month, we begin to persuade them to buy a home. As soon as they save enough money for the first payment, the bank will help them out. There is this woman who came to us eighteen years ago. She did odd jobs and we paid her a dollar a week, which she was glad to get. But we encouraged her to fit herself for better things. She studied, took a business course at night school and has worked her way up until now she is our head book-

keeper with a salary of one hundred and fifty dollars a month. She has a nice home, well-furnished and fully paid for, and she has money in the bank!"

Maggie fully understood the importance of knowing how money could be put to work by women as well as men, blacks as well as whites, to make more money. She refused to be hemmed in by what she called "spheres," or roles for women. These were the roles which society had designated for women to keep them in their place. When questioned about how she could afford to spend so much time out of the home, she quipped, *"[My] household is so well organized that I want something more to do beyond domesticity and the social whirl."* Redefining those spheres became her mission. Working away from the home was Maggie's way of breaking down the barriers of prejudice against women in the workplace. Of course, being bank president and manager of one of the most successful fraternal organizations in the country helped her make her point. Women could see through her example that a woman could be successful, if given the opportunity.

"Whatever has come in these days has come to

*Maggie always worked hard, even after she was
confined to a wheelchair due to ill health.*

me, because I have worked from a child; worked before I married, worked after I married, and am working now harder than I ever worked in my life," she said.

Though she was interested in prejudice against women in general, she was especially concerned about the double jeopardy or double limitations placed on blacks by virtue of race. *"Our Negro women [are] hemmed in, circumscribed with every imaginable obstacles [sic] in our way, blocked and held down by the fears and prejudices of the whites—ridiculed and sneered at by the intelligent blacks,"* she wrote.

Maggie Walker used her sphere of influence in the business community to encourage blacks to go into business, and to "buy black," particularly when she was establishing the St. Luke Emporium. The Emporium was a small, neighborhood department store with a "complete line of up-to-date stock direct from the New York market." The Emporium carried hats, shoes, men and womens' clothing, and cloth. It flourished for four years amidst stiff competition. When Maggie was asked to speak at the Hampton Negro Conference in 1905 as a businesswoman, she made it a point to encourage blacks to buy from other Negroes, and keep the money in their communities.

Maggie Walker didn't just call others to action. She was a woman of action herself. She organized the local chapter of the National Council of Colored Women. She was a charter member of the National Association for the Advancement of Colored People. She was on the board of the Industrial School for Girls which her dear friend, Janie Porter Barrett, founded. She raised funds for the school, and gave money out of her own pocket to keep the school running. She was also a member of the Women's League, which was later responsible for the establishment of the first black hospital in Richmond. With each new project and each new idea for improvement, Maggie's sphere of influence widened.

✥ 15 ✥
"The Rainiest Day"

110½ East Leigh Street had been a beehive of activity for years. At one time, four generations of family lived together under one roof: Maggie and Armstead; Elizabeth Mitchell; Russell and his wife Hattie and their daughter Maggie Laura; Melvin and Ethel and their three children: Mamie Evelyn, Armstead, and Elizabeth. The children had filled the house with scurrying footsteps and peals of mischievous laughter. Since there was no television, the family read or listened to the radio. Sometimes they would gather to talk and to share stories.

In 1921, Russell was diagnosed with tuberculosis. His mother arranged for him to go to Canada with Dr. Hughes for treatment. His last Christmas was undoubtedly one of the saddest.

"My not writing home to you wasn't because I haven't thought of you and home, but I imagine

At one time, several generations had lived under one roof. Russell and daughter Maggie Laura at left; Maggie Walker and her mother, Elizabeth Mitchell, in center; Melvin and son Armstead at right.

you, like God, get tired of people's complaints. Especially when the same people seem to forget you in their prosperity," he wrote to his mother. He never fully recovered from the bout with tuberculosis or from his father's death. Despite the loving efforts of his mother, his wife Hattie, and his daughter Maggie Laura, he had become very depressed. He drank too much. He had been a first-class accountant. Now, he was working in a doctor's office in Brooklyn, New York, and even that meager job had come to an abrupt end on Christmas Eve.

Maggie's beloved mother, Elizabeth Draper Mitchell, who had been a slave, a servant, and a washerwoman, had died on February 12, 1922. The next year Russell died on November 23, 1923. Within seven years Maggie had lost her husband, her mother, and now her oldest son.

As the first grandchild, Maggie Laura had been given her grandmother's name. She was born and raised in her grandmother's house. There she had been surrounded by a nurturing family of aunts, uncle, and cousins. Maggie Laura and her grandmother shared so many memories. How many times had she crawled into the huge four-poster bed to be close to her grandma? They

would talk about everything, even about Maggie
Laura's boyfriends. They had loved each other so
much. They had been such good friends.

Now her grandmother was finding it increasingly difficult to bear the pain in her leg. She had
injured her kneecap in 1907. She had tried many
remedies, including visiting Hot Springs, Arkansas, for a cure. In her journal of April 30, 1921,
she had noted: *April was spent in Arkansas. Feeling fine after 21 hot baths and four massages.*

But the relief was temporary. After a while,
the doctor fitted Maggie Walker for leg braces.
She found them cumbersome. Yet, she continued
to work diligently and remained in good spirits,
sustained by her unwavering faith in God, her
supportive family, and friends.

Maggie Laura watched her grandmother live
with the pain and inconvenience of her disability
as her condition worsened and she was confined
to a wheelchair. It was Polly who suggested that
they install an elevator in the rear of the house.
Now Miss Maggie would be able to get up and
down without much trouble. She also had her
car adjusted so that the wheelchair could fit
into it.

When her grandmother's last hours came,

Maggie Laura was in the middle of a piano lesson at Mrs. Evelyn Frazier's house. A neighbor summoned her to come home at once. Her grandmother had taken a turn for the worse. As Maggie Laura raced to the house, her heart pounded with uncertainty:

"When he got me home, she was in a coma. And they thought if I would call her, and if anybody could bring her out of it, I would be able to. And I can distinctly remember sitting there the rest of the day, saying, 'Grandmom, Grandmom, Grandmom,' you know, halfway crying and halfway trying to get her to—and she didn't respond. And Dr. Hughes was in and out, and several of the physicians were in and out, you know, trying to do whatever it is that they do at the last minute. There were certainly no respirators in those days, you know, those drastic procedures, and she died in bed . . ."

It was December 15, 1934 when Maggie Lena Walker died. The official cause of death was diabetic gangrene. As was customary, the body remained in the parlor of her home. It is said that thousands of people came through to view her body. News of her death sent shock waves of disbelief and sadness throughout the country. Messages and condolences were received from everywhere. Her native city of Richmond stopped to give homage to this great lady. Lampposts were draped in black. White and black businesses alike flew their flags at half-mast. Even the colored schools were closed for a half-day so that young people could pay their final respects.

"It was the rainiest day that I ever had witnessed. I got soaking wet," recalled Dan Perkins, a youngster who attended the funeral. He had often helped push Mrs. Walker's wheelchair up the ramp to the First African Baptist Church. Now he wanted to pay his respects. When he arrived at the church, it was already overflowing with people. Hundreds of people stood out in the pouring rain. Luckily Dan was able to sit in the balcony. He was nervous that his damp clothes were not good enough, and might smell from the rain. But then he thought, Mrs. Walker would not have cared if he smelled! She had only cared about what was important and good for people. As the choir sang, Dan cried.

In a letter to the *Richmond News Leader*, Maggie Walker's friend, Nannie Burroughs, wrote eloquently:

I have traveled the country over and I have attended funerals of many noted colored Americans, but I have never seen such sincere evidence of appreciation and love on the part of public officials, including the police force, in all my life. . . . I know I express the desire of millions of our people when I say that we extend to you, to the fine white people of Richmond, the deepest gratitude of our hearts and a rising vote of thanks for wiping out the color line and giving unstinted honor and praise to the woman who gave her life as a ransom for many.

Epilogue

Maggie Lena Walker was buried in Evergreen Cemetery. Even months after the funeral, memorials were held by various organizations. Under a portrait of Maggie Walker, the *Richmond Planet* reminded its readers:

> As a memorial to Mrs. Maggie L. Walker, who spent her life trying to enhance the political and civil fortunes of her people, pay your poll taxes by December 2, 1935.

Even before her death, the Order had commissioned J.S. Collins to create a bust to memorialize Maggie Walker. Replicas of the white plaster bust adorned mantles, tables, and piano tops in the parlors of Negro homes. Another lasting memorial was the new high school that would be named for her, by unanimous decision of the Richmond City school board. It was revealed that Mrs. Walker had given a $10,000 loan to the city, during lean times, so that the school year would not be curtailed for Negro children.

Like so many "race women" of her generation, she was a warrior. Maggie Walker's sisterhood included Lillian H. Payne, Patsie K. Anderson, Ella O. Waller, Mary Church Terrell, Ida B. Wells Barnett, Nannie H. Burroughs, Mary McCleod Bethune, Janie Porter Barrett, and hundreds of unsung heroines. They attacked the conventional wisdom that Negroes and women could not take care of themselves. They took strides beyond the roles that had been designated "for colored only." They had to fend off the two-headed monster of racism and sexism.

Maggie Walker was one of many stars in the constellations of women who light up the world. This light is an eternal flame for hope and justice.

The light was passed on by a group of dedicated people who founded the Maggie L. Walker Historical Foundation in 1974 to acquire and preserve the Maggie Walker House and legacy. On July 15, 1979, the Walker family presented the deed to the Maggie Walker house at 110½ East Leigh Street, Richmond, to the United States National Park Service. The house has been preserved along with several homes and buildings in the neighborhood which have been restored to their previous glory. They stand as a National Historic Site, now used to convey and to interpret the works and times of this magnificent woman and her community. Maggie Walker's words of encouragement live on as sound advice: "Have faith; have courage; and carry on."

Index

(Page numbers in boldface indicate captions or photographs.)